Not Ethan Again!

Written by

Sally Prue

Illustrated by

Jenni Desmond

OXFORD
UNIVERSITY PRESS

OXFORD
UNIVERSITY PRESS

Great Clarendon Street, Oxford, OX2 6DP, United Kingdom

Oxford University Press is a department of the University
of Oxford. It furthers the University's objective of excellence
in research, scholarship, and education by publishing
worldwide. Oxford is a registered trade mark of Oxford
University Press in the UK and in certain other countries

Text © Sally Prue 2015
Illustrations © Jenni Desmond 2015

The moral rights of the author have been asserted

First published 2015

British Library Cataloguing in Publication Data
Data available

ISBN: 978-0-19-835645-5

10

Paper used in the production of this book is a natural, recyclable product
made from wood grown in sustainable forests. The manufacturing process
conforms to the environmental regulations of the country of origin.

Printed in China by Shanghai Offset Printing Products Ltd

Acknowledgements

Series Advisor: Nikki Gamble

Jessie had the most annoying big brother in the world. Ethan was nine, which was two years older than Jessie. He was *always* taking Jessie's stuff.

When Jessie's scooter went missing, she knew at once who had taken it. She searched for her scooter everywhere.

It wasn't by the door.

It wasn't in the garden.

By the time Jessie heard scooter wheels on the pavement outside, she was really cross.

Ethan was showing off to Samantha and her friends.
He was *always* showing off to Samantha.

He looked really silly.

He looked even **more** silly when he

crashed

into a bush.

Jessie rushed back into the house.

"Mum!" she said. "Ethan took my scooter again!"

"Oh Jessie, I wish you'd stop moaning," said Mum.

"Stop *moaning*? But he's broken one of the wheels!" said Jessie.

"Oh dear," said Mum. "He's not hurt, is he?"

"My scooter's the thing that's hurt," said Jessie. "Now I won't be able to show Granny how well I ride. She's coming for her birthday in two days!"

"Well, perhaps I'll have a look at it when I get a spare moment," said Mum.

The next day was boring. Jessie's scooter was broken and there was nothing to do.

"Tell you what," said Dad. "Why don't you make a birthday card for Granny?"

"Yes, she'd really like that!" said Jessie.

Jessie painted a very good picture of Granny on the card.

She put it by the window to dry and went to wash her hands.

But when she came back, the card was nowhere to be seen.

"Not Ethan again!" shouted Jessie. She rushed out into the garden.

But she was too late. Ethan was giving Samantha the card.

Samantha sniffed when she saw it.

"I don't have grey hair, Ethan," she said. "*Or* wrinkles. And I'm not seventy, either!"

"Mum!" called Jessie. "Ethan took Granny's card!"

"Oh Jessie, stop moaning," said Mum.

"But he's written on the card and ruined it!" said Jessie.

Ethan scowled. "Silly card," he said crossly. "I'll get Samantha something loads better than that!"

"Just leave my stuff alone," said Jessie.

Ethan grabbed Jessie's fishing net and went out.

"It's not *fair!*" said Jessie. "I can't show Granny how well I ride my scooter, and now her card's spoiled, too."

"We'll make Granny some jam instead," said Dad. "Granny loves home-made jam. As she's going to be seventy, let's make seven jars – one for every ten years."

Jessie and Dad spent ages washing the fruit and stirring it.

But then …

"Where's that last jam jar gone?" asked Dad.

Jessie knew straight away. She pointed out of the window.

"There!" she shouted. "It's Ethan again!"

Ethan was giving the jar to Samantha. It had a frog in it.

Samantha didn't seem to like frogs very much.

"**Eeeeeeek!**" she screamed.

"What's all that noise?" asked Mum, coming in.

"It's Ethan again!" said Jessie. "He's taken the seventh jam jar. He's—"

"Oh Jessie, stop moaning," said Mum.

"Stop *moaning*? But now we haven't got enough jars for the jam!" said Jessie. "And Granny's coming tomorrow!"

The only jar they could find was an empty hair gel jar.

"Granny won't mind having jam in a jar with **Hair Gel** written on the lid," said Dad.

"Ethan spoils *everything*," said Jessie.

"Well, you'll have to make sure he *doesn't* get the chance to spoil this," said Dad.

Jessie thought very carefully about how to keep
Granny's jam safe. That night she hid all seven jars
in her bedroom.

When she woke up the next morning, she left
the curtains closed so the room stayed dark.

But when she came back from the bathroom …

"**Put that down!**"
howled Jessie.

Ethan took no notice.

He opened the hair gel jar, scooped out a huge glob of sticky jam ... and put it on his hair.

"Mum!" shouted Jessie. "Ethan's—"

"Oh Jessie, stop moaning," said Mum.

Jessie opened her mouth – and then she stopped and closed her mouth again.

Ethan's hair was red with jam, but Jessie didn't say a word.

Outside, Samantha stared
at Ethan in surprise.

"What have you
done to your hair?"
she asked. "And what's
that buzzing sound?"

21

Ethan looked around. There were a
lot of wasps about and they were all
flying straight towards him.

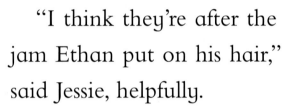

"I think they're after the
jam Ethan put on his hair,"
said Jessie, helpfully.
"Jam?" said Ethan.
"*Jam?*" said Samantha.

Ethan ran a finger
through his hair.
He licked his finger.

"**Aarrgghhh!**"

Ethan screamed.

He ran away as fast as he could.

Jessie watched him happily. She was sure it would be a *really* long time before Ethan took any of her stuff again.